COSMO *girl!*

Words
to
Live By

COSMO girl!

Words to Live By

From The Editors of *CosmoGIRL!*

**Hearst Books
A Division of Sterling
Publishing Co., Inc.
New York**

Library of Congress Cataloging-in-Publication Data

CosmoGirl! : words to live by / from the editors of Cosmo girl.
    p. cm.
  Includes index.
  Audience: Ages 15 & up.
  ISBN 1-58816-528-0
  1. Conduct of life—Quotations, maxims, etc. 2. Girls—Quotations. 3.
Women—Quotations. I. Title: Cosmo girl!. II. Cosmo girl.
  PN6084.C556C68 2006
  305.4—dc22

                                    2005023600

Book design by Margaret Rubiano

CosmoGIRL! and Hearst Books are registered trademarks of
Hearst Communications, Inc.

www.cosmogirl.com

For information about custom editions, special sales, premium and
corporate purchases, please contact Sterling Special Sales Department at
800-805-5489 or specialsales@sterlingpub.com.

Distributed in Canada by Sterling Publishing
c/o Canadian Manda Group, 165 Dufferin Street
Toronto, Ontario, Canada M6K 3H6

Distributed in Australia by Capricorn Link (Australia) Pty. Ltd.
P.O. Box 704, Windsor, NSW 2756 Australia

Printed in China

Sterling ISBN 13: 978-1-58816-528-2
        ISBN 10: 1-58816-528-0

Contents

From Me to You

Everyone's got a favorite quote that they like to remember to guide them through life—something that reminds you of your power, your confidence, your strength. Since *CosmoGIRL!* is all about helping you, our readers, to find those things within yourself, we're always on the lookout for great mantras that can inspire you to be your best. Every month, whether we're giving advice on how to pursue your dreams, or asking your favorite celebs to tell you what keeps them motivated, or prompting you to send in stories of what inspires you, we pack *CosmoGIRL!* full of sayings that can energize you physically, mentally, and spiritually. Sometimes these quotes are just fun little pick-me-ups, sometimes they're deeper and more thought-provoking, and sometimes they're a little bit in between. But no matter which way you read this book, I know you'll find at least a few words here that really speak to you. You can read through it all at once, or keep it on your night table to take like a vitamin, swallowing just a little morsel of wisdom to guide you each day. Sometimes one quote might jump out at you during a certain time in your life, and then a few months later, there's a completely different one that you feel helps you overcome the obstacles and keep your eye on your prize. But each quote is like a gem, and I want you to know that they've been strung together in this compilation like a beautiful jewel necklace designed specially for you, CosmoGIRL!—a girl who lives her life her way, who makes her mark on her community, and who causes a ripple effect of optimism to flow out to the rest of the world. Thank you for your creativity, your hope, and your love—you are truly special, and these quotes are for you! Email me anytime with new ones that you love at susan@cosmogirl.com. Enjoy!

Love,

Susan

COSMO girl!

it's a girl thing

{ *Being a girl is about being strong. It's about realizing you have the power to let your opinions and your voice be heard. It's about getting attention, not for your body, but for your heart and mind.* }

"I'm not going around kicking ass. But it's nice to know I can."
—Jessica Alba, actor

"We have curves and no matter what anyone says, we are beautiful."
—Brittany, 16, CG! reader

"The best compliment a man can pay a woman is to say she thinks like a woman."
—Margaret Thatcher, former British prime minister

"Women have every right. They only have to exercise them."
—Victoria Woodhull, first female U.S. presidential candidate, 1872

"Girls have the power to come together with so many creative ideas and new ways of doing things. Without girl power, the world would be a colder, darker place."
—Katie, 14, CG! reader

"Learn to enjoy your own personal beauty. You might have a big nose, but so what? It's your nose. Love your short hair or your big cheeks!"
—Usher, singer, actor

"When I stopped saying 'I look awful,' I recognized that I could be beautiful."
—Laura Mercier, makeup artist

"If you wouldn't do it to a baby's face, don't do it to your own."
—Dr. Marsha Gordon, dermatologist

"The ultimate in girl power: having the opportunity to bring another human being into the world—when we're older!"
—Taylor, 17, CG! reader

17

"If you want anything said, ask a man. If you want anything done, ask a woman."
—Margaret Thatcher, former British prime minister

"The thing women have got to learn is that nobody gives you power. You just take it."
—Roseanne Barr, actor

"Be a strong female—don't be afraid of the flack that goes along with that."
—Christina Aguilera, singer-songwriter

"What I have to say is more important than how long my lashes are."
—Alanis Morissette, singer-songwriter

"The thing I love best about being a girl is that we're more open than guys. We can talk about our problems and feelings to other women."
—Angela, 16, CG! reader

"I do care how I look, because I'm a girl, but I don't want people to listen with their eyes."
—Joss Stone, singer-songwriter

"A woman who truly believes in herself—that's a powerful kind of beauty."
—**Sonia Kashuk, makeup artist**

"Women should be proud of their bodies and not dis others for being proud of theirs."
—Christina Aguilera, singer-songwriter

"A woman is like a tea bag—only in hot water do you realize how strong she is."
—**Eleanor Roosevelt, former first lady, humanitarian**

"There is a woman at the beginning of all great things."
—Alphonse de Lamartine, French politician and poet

> **"Being grateful to your body is the key to loving yourself."**
> **—Oprah Winfrey**

> "A girl wants to look sexy. But what's important is that people take you seriously as a human."
> —Gwen Stefani, singer-songwriter

> **"Being strong physically and mentally is beautiful."**
> **—Jessica Biel, actor**

23

"Women are the real architects of society."
—Harriet Beecher Stowe, author

"A woman can bear you, break you, take you."
—Queen Latifah, rapper, actor

"A woman must have money and a room of her own."
—Virginia Woolf, author

"One shouldn't expect privileges because of her sex. Neither should she adjust to prejudice."
—Betty Friedan, author

"Good girls go to heaven; bad girls go everywhere."
—Helen Gurley Brown, author, publisher, editor-in-chief of the international editions of Cosmopolitan

"If you think you look and feel good, keep it up—and don't let anyone change your mind!"
—Susan Schulz, CosmoGIRL! editor-in-chief

"Women are the one group who grow more radical with age."
—Gloria Steinem, author, activist

"I do not wish (women) to have power over men, but over themselves."
—Mary Wollstonecraft Shelley, author

"Being able to enjoy being a woman—and showing [it]—is so powerful."
—Catherine Zeta-Jones, actor

"Well-behaved women rarely make history."
—Laurel Thatcher Ulrich, author, historian

"Women never have young minds. They are born 3,000 years old."
—**Shelagh Delaney, playwright**

"I feel beautiful because of my heart. It really doesn't have anything to do with my physical features."
—Lauryn Hill, singer-songwriter

"I just want equal rights for boys and girls. That's what feminism is to me."
—**Billie Jean King, athlete**

"We are volcanoes. When we women offer our experiences as truth...there are new mountains."
—Ursula K. Le Guin, author

"After all, God made man and then said, 'I can do better than that'—and made woman."
—Adela Rogers St. Johns, journalist

"**Educate a woman and you can educate a family.**"
—Jovit Idar, founder of The League of Mexican Women

"Wake up every day and look in the mirror and say 'Damn, you look hot' and leave the house with that in your head to carry with you all day."
—Elizabeth, 18, CG! reader

"Sex appeal is 50 percent of what you've got and 50 percent of what people think you've got."
—Sophia Loren, actor

"Makeup is only the icing on the cake—it doesn't create your personality or your being."
—Sonia Kashuk, makeup artist

"Why not be oneself? That is the whole secret of a successful appearance."
—Edith Sitwell, poet

"Women's place is in the House—and in the Senate."
—Gloria Schaffer, former Connecticut secretary of state

"People call me a feminist when my sensibilities differentiate me from a doormat."
—Rebecca West, author

"One is not born a woman, one becomes one."
—Simone de Beauvoir, author

"Realize that you don't have to follow trends—differences can become your signature."
—Dayle Haddon, model, author

"Women should run the world. They should be presidents, kings, and queens, and that should be the end of it."
—Jon Bon Jovi, singer-songwriter

> **"The less we do with our hair, the happier we are."**
> **—Orlando Pita, hairstylist**

"Flaws often become the very things that make us beautiful."
—Rachel Urquhart, beauty expert

☆

"As girls we should embrace our bodies and the beauty of it—all of it."
—Amber, 17, CG! reader

"I'm very into embracing your flaws and knowing that you're beautiful for a lot of different reasons besides just what you look like on the outside."
—Hilary Duff, actor, singer

"The beauty I love is in people who look real."
—Calvin Klein, designer

"You are what you are, you know? I don't look in the mirror and say 'Oh, I'm the most beautiful girl in the world. Look at me.' I see my imperfections. I just don't care."
—Kelly Osbourne, actor, singer

"There's still this negativity towards women who use an inherent strength—femininity—in ways that are considered seductive."
—Demi Moore, actor

"Just because I change my hair doesn't mean I change my soul."
—Faith Hill, singer-songwriter, actor

"I've seen women all over this planet changing communities and transforming the way people think."

—Eve Ensler, playwright, activist

☆

"When I was a teenager, there were times I felt insecure about my looks. I thought I was a little pudgy, and I believed that my legs were too big and my body was too muscular. At some point it dawned on me that this is the body God gave me and I have to love and appreciate it."

—Serena Williams, athlete

"I don't think anyone can teach you how to be a man but a woman."
—Ryan Gosling, actor

**"I maintain that at the root of glamour, there's confidence."
—Isaac Mizrahi, designer**

"If you think you ought to be physically perfect you might never find out that you're useful for all the right reasons—and not all those stupid things that people tell you you're useful for."
—Angelina Jolie, actor, humanitarian

"Perfection is boring. If a face doesn't have some mistakes, it's nothing."
—Kevyn Aucoin, makeup artist

"Lots of girls struggle with their weight. But, being skinny doesn't necessarily mean being happy."
—Stephanie, 16, CG! reader

Inspiring Advice You Can Use Every Day!

The seven secrets of truly beautiful girls: Get lots of sleep. Drink a lot of water. Love your hair as it is, curly or straight. Don't smoke. Eat well. Work out regularly. And most important—love yourself. Happiness and confidence simply radiate beauty.

Sometimes what you want to say gets lost in how you say it. Don't say "I'll try...I'm not sure but...I guess...I think...or: I could be wrong." Say "I will... I'm positive...this is my opinion...and: I know." If you sound like you believe yourself, other people will too!

Following the cliquey girls at school can be tempting. But showing people your real personality gives you power. You can either let other people take the lead and then follow. Or you can live by your own rules because you already are likeable, respectable, and very, very cool. Own it!

Be nice, nice, nice is what they tell us from the time we're little. And it's not bad to be nice or modest—the world would be a much better place if everyone played by those rules. But not everyone does. So learn to stand up, find your voice, and grab some power!

COSMO girl!

love lines

Everyone has a first love story. So if you don't, that only means you haven't had a first love yet, and that you have one of life's most exciting milestones awaiting you!

"I've learned your heart is tucked deep into your chest for a reason. You should never let anybody take it out and throw it around."
—Cheyanne, 16, CG! reader

"Love does not consist of gazing at each other, but in looking outward together in the same direction."
—Antoine de Saint-Exupéry, poet, writer

"If a guy's into you, he'll ignore his cell phone when you're around because there's no one else he'd rather talk to."
—Lee, 20, CG! reader

"Girls get so caught up in trying to please guys. If the guy you want doesn't want you, he ain't the one for you anyway. Don't settle!"
—**Usher, singer, actor**

45

"After a bad relationship I vowed not to get caught up in the idea of love, but to hold out for a guy who'd treat me right and be right for me. Now I know I have the real thing. We really got to know each other first and, over time, fell more and more in love."
—Maggie, 21, CG! reader

"...whosoever loves much performs much, and can accomplish much, and what is done in love is done well."
—Vincent van Gogh, artist

"Love has given me wings so I must fly."
—Sir William Thatcher, (Heath Ledger), A Knight's Tale

47

"Give yourself credit for knowing who you are and what you want—you can date a guy without being brainwashed by him and chucking everything you've worked for in your life."
—CosmoGIRL! editor

"At this point in my life, I really do want a serious relationship. But I'm not one to go out and pick a random apple—it has to be sweet and clean for me. So I'm going to wait for the right guy."
—Sarah, 16, CG! reader

"I'd rather spend one minute holding you than the rest of my life knowing I never could."
—**Jimmy (Jake Gyllenhaal), Bubble Boy**

"If you don't want to be with yourself, why should anyone else?"
—Meghan, 16, CG! reader

"I may not be a smart man, but I know what love is."
—Forrest (Tom Hanks), Forrest Gump

"When we find someone whose weirdness is compatible with ours, we join them in mutual weirdness and call it love—true love."
—**Robert Fulgham, author**

"I kept my last relationship on the down low for three weeks to give us time to get to know each other without anyone skewing our view with their opinions."
—Denise, 21, CG! reader

"The faster a relationship moves, the less time it will last. If you jump straight into making out or sex, you'll have nothing to look forward to. I respect a girl who wants to take it slow and sticks to her guns about it."
—Matthew, 19

"Love is a fruit in season at all times, and within reach of every hand."
—Mother Teresa, nun, humanitarian

"**Death cannot stop true love. All it can do is delay it for a while.**"
—**Westley (Cary Elwes), The Princess Bride**

"You don't love someone for their looks, or their clothes, or for their fancy car, but because they sing a song only you can hear."
—Anonymous

"**The love we give away is the only love we keep.**"
—**Elbert Hubbard, writer**

> "**Nice** guys are refreshing. And witnessing their warm-hearted ways is actually pretty hot!"
> —**CosmoGIRL!** editor

"When you find her, fight for her...because in your heart you know that the juice is worth the squeeze."
—Matthew (Emile Hirsch),
The Girl Next Door

"This is the miracle that happens every time to those who really love: The more they give, the more they possess."
—**Rainer Maria Rilke, poet**

"A kiss blown is a kiss wasted. The only real kiss is a kiss tasted!"
—Pete, 17

"Whenever you get to the point where you know you don't need a boyfriend, then you will be ready for one!"
—Traci, 15, CG! reader

"I'm in love with love. It's heavenly when you're falling for someone and you can't stop thinking about her."
—Orlando Bloom, actor

**"It is only in the mysterious equations of love that any logical reasons can be found."
—John Nash (Russell Crowe), A Beautiful Mind**

"If you look for it, I've got a sneaky feeling that love actually is all around."
—Prime Minister of England (Hugh Grant), Love Actually

> **"Did you ever put your arms out and spin and spin and spin? Well, that's what love is like."**
> **—Gillian Owens (Nicole Kidman), Practical Magic**

"No one ever really dies from a broken heart."
—Patrice, 21, CG! reader

"That moment when you kiss someone and everything around becomes hazy...you get this amazing gift."
—**Josie (Drew Barrymore), Never Been Kissed**

"My first time...I was in love, but I wish I had waited longer. If I were older, I think I would have enjoyed it more."
—Mirka, 17, CG! reader

"We cannot really love anybody with whom we never laugh."
—**Agnes Repplier, essayist**

"Dating a friend is like starting on the tenth date. You already know so much about each other, but there's still a newness for both of you since it's your first time going down this road together."
—Colleen, 21, CG! reader

"Everyone is searching for similar things out of life—and there's a quiet comfort that comes from reminding yourself that you're not alone in your quest for true love."
—CosmoGIRL! **editor**

"I thought sex was this big deal and that I was the only one not doing it, but once I did, I realized I could have waited until the time was right."
—Tim, 21

"A guy wants a girl who is confident and shows she's independent and doesn't always need him."
—Lindsay Lohan, actor, singer

"You can't help who you love; you're not supposed to."
—Chenille (Kerry Washington),
Save the Last Dance

"Our love is like the wind. I can't see it, but I can feel it."
—Landon (Shane West), A Walk to Remember

"Love is not finding the perfect person, it's seeing an imperfect person perfectly."
Autumn, 15, CG! reader

"Where there is great love, there are always miracles."
—Willa Cather, writer

"It's great to be young and have fun, but I don't hook up with random people. I'm careful not to cross that line. I want something serious."
—Avril Lavigne, singer-songwriter

"I feel that what's meant for me will wait for me."
—Usher, singer, actor

> "That's why they call them crushes. If they were easy, we'd call them something else."
> —**Jim Baker (Paul Dooley),** Sixteen Candles

> "No guy is worth crying over, and if he is, he won't make you cry."
> —Priscilla, 16, CG! reader

> "Everyone wants to ride in the limo—you want someone who'll take the bus with you if the limo breaks down."
> —Oprah Winfrey

"I think everyone has a soul mate. But I don't think you can attract one until you say, I'm cool by myself."
—Madonna, singer-songwriter, actor

"Never let any guy, no matter where he falls on the "good" scale, make you feel any kind of bad."
—CosmoGIRL! editor

"I love it when I see a girl who can laugh really loud and not care who's watching her."
—Adam, 17

"Why be with someone who doesn't really want to be with you?"
—Jennifer Love-Hewitt, actor, singer

"A guy might be able to slow me down, but he's not going to break me."

—Toni Braxton, singer

"You don't need to go further than kissing to have a meaningful relationship."

—Sheyda, 18, CG! reader

"Guys are emotional; they just don't know exactly how to express their feelings. And a lot of girls interpret that as being shut off. You've just got to give it some time. Guys need to feel comfortable and trust the person they're with."
—Nick Lachey, singer

"I started giving good guys a chance. Turns out they're not needy—they're respectful. Now it's those guys I pay attention to!"
—Tracy, 18, CG! reader

"I want a girl who has opinions, reads the newspaper, or is in some way knowledgeable and interested in things beyond herself."
—Jamie, 21, CG! reader

"I really get into a relationship when I'm in one. But if a guy's not calling, he's not worth it."
—Avril Lavigne, singer-songwriter

"Two years ago I swore off casually making out. It's hard not to give in to temptation, but now when I hook up with a guy, I feel in control—empowered—because I know he really likes me."
—Emily, 19, CG! reader

"Relationships are a mystery. They don't get easier as you get older, but you should always fall in love with your whole heart."
—Katie Holmes, actor

"If you don't respect yourself and love yourself the way you should—if you don't realize your own value and worth—then somebody else will see that and take advantage of it."
—Kelly Rowland, singer

"My life is too important to waste time pining over a guy who doesn't want to be with me."
—Staci, 17, CG! reader

"When you fall in love, it just makes you so much more aware of everything."
—Kirsten Dunst, actor

"Smart is sexy. When a girl can talk about things other than the last mall she went to or who's dating who."
—John, 20

"I think when you find the right thing, in many ways, what you want out of them will be what they want to give you....figure out what it is that you want to give somebody else—and then find that person."

—Ashton Kutcher, actor

Inspiring Advice You Can Use Every Day!

Think of love—and the pain of breaking up—as exercise for your heart. The pain is tough, true. But it only means your heart is getting stronger.

Need more romance? If you feel like you're doing all of the giving and none of the receiving, you probably are. So lead by example by subtly teaching him how to give you the attention you want. Show him that you're thinking of him in meaningful ways and inspire him to do the same for you. Just don't let him take your sweet gestures for granted!

Don't postpone a breakup because you feel guilty—you'll feel less guilty once you end it for good and let him move on too!

You know how the type of guy you're attracted to sometimes stink in a relationships? If you lock yourself into a specific type too soon, you miss out on the great unknown of what might be better for you. Expand your horizons and really learn about guys, love and yourself.

COSMO girl!

spirit

{ Your spirit gives you power and guidance—it urges you to follow your heart. It is the truth of who you are. And when you honor it, you'll feel stronger, happier, and more at peace with yourself—and others. }

"Who would ever think that so much went on in the soul of a young girl?"
—Anne Frank, diarist

"The cookie-cutter image of beauty is not beautiful, but quirks are beautiful."
—Julia Stiles, actor

"Look at life sunny-side up!"
—Laura, 15, CG! reader

"Loving ourselves works miracles in our lifetime."
—**Louise L. Hay, author**

"If you make peace with yourself, you'll feel at peace with others."
—Holly, 15, CG! reader

"Discovering who you are, independent of anyone [else] is the hardest work of all."
—Janet Jackson, singer-songwriter

"We truly are all champions in our own ways."
—Kaitlin, 14, CG! reader

"I don't want to be the next anybody. I want to be the first me!"
— Natalie Imbruglia, singer-songwriter

"Why do people do yoga? To clear their minds? I embrace the clutter in my head."
—**Chris Rock, comedian**

"I don't judge others. I say, if you feel good with what you're doing, let your freak flag fly!"
—Sarah Jessica Parker, actor

"It's okay to make a fool of yourself, but do it with confidence."
—Ina, 16, CG! reader

"Nobody has a better vision of who you are than yourself."
—Sheryl Crow, singer-songwriter

"A sister filled with joy preaches without preaching."
—Mother Teresa, nun, humanitarian

"It's great, when you've looked to others for happiness…to realize you can give yourself that feeling."
—Drew Barrymore, actor, producer

"I believe strongly in my own personal magic."
—Susan Sarandon, actor

"Don't think less of yourself, think of yourself less."
—Julie, 15, CG! reader

"Looking like you is the best thing. It makes you unique, because there's nobody else on the face of the Earth that looks like you. Nobody."
—Beyoncé Knowles, singer, actor

"Sit on the grass and watch the sun set. There's something about that sort of beauty that can help you forget your worries and remember how precious life really is."
—Gloria, 14, CG! reader

> "Enjoy who you are. Don't hate yourself for what you aren't."
> —**Heather Graham, actor**

"Letting loose and being who you really are helps you feel free. My friends tell me how weird I am—and how happy they are to have me as a friend!"
—Lexi, 18, CG! reader

"Though we travel the world over to find the beautiful, we must carry it with us or we find it not."
—Ralph Waldo Emerson, writer

"Beauty is not in the face; beauty is a light in the heart."
—Kahlil Gibran, poet

"Calmness of mind is one of the most beautiful jewels of wisdom."
—Jessie, 19, CG! reader

> **"Everything has its beauty, but not everyone sees it."**
> **—Confucius, philosopher**

"Confidence begins when you define your own style and enjoy who you are."
—Susie Galvez, author

"Be strong, be bold, be unique. Be anything you want to be!"
—Bonnika, 16, CG! reader

"I grew up in the projects, but I was never poor in spirit."

—Mary J. Blige, singer-songwriter

"I'm only young once, so who cares if I'm a goofball?"

—Haley, 16, CG! reader

"The light always shows on the outside if you are striving to be good inside."

—Erykah Badu, singer-songwriter

"I don't put my self-worth in anyone else's hands,"
—Kristin, 21, CG! reader

"Spending time alone…those are some of the best moments."
—Alicia Keys, singer-songwriter

"There's something liberating about not pretending. Dare to embarrass yourself."
—Drew Barrymore, actor, producer

"Trust yourself. You know yourself better than anyone else."
—Juicy, 17, CG! reader

"Remember to delight yourself first, then others will be truly delighted."
—SARK, author, illustrator

"No pessimist ever discovered the secrets of the stars or sailed to an uncharted land."
—Helen Keller, author

"Out of your vulnerabilities will come your strength."
—Sigmund Freud, psychologist

"Everybody has to have faith in something. Some put it in God or a higher power; I have faith in myself."
—Jewlia, 14, CG! reader

"Optimism is a choice. Cynicism isn't smarter, it's just safer."
—Jewel, singer-songwriter

"Find what is unique about you. If someone doesn't like it, don't change. Someone else eventually will."

—Kelly Clarkson, singer-songwriter

"Be emotional, extreme, intense overwhelming.... Be all those things and more, because the world is lacking in passion and people who put themselves on the line to change the world."

—Eve Ensler, playwright and activist

"I'm still a 6-year-old-kid. I always will be, and I think that's an important thing to hold on to."
—Heath Ledger, actor

"You have to stand for what you believe in. And sometimes you have to stand alone."
—Queen Latifah, rapper, actor

"I don't believe you should make fun of anyone but yourself."
—Cameron Diaz, actor

"What makes you valuable is your heart...and how you present yourself to the world."
—Jada Pinkett-Smith, actor, singer

"I just had to be more of me instead of just some of me."
—Pink, singer-songwriter

"You don't have to be a star...to feel good. It's not always about being the biggest, tallest, strongest. It's about the fight and fire within you."
—Jennie Finch, pro softball player

"People say don't judge a book by its cover. I say don't judge it at all."
—Sara-Mai, 14, CG! reader

"Everyone feels like a dork sometimes. And just admitting it can make you laugh and feel like, 'Hey, it's who I am. Deal with it, people!'"
—Susan Schulz, CosmoGIRL! editor-in-chief

"Try something new and exciting and have as much fun as you can. You don't have to be great at (it), just be willing to have a great time!"
—**Venus Williams, athlete**

"Free spirits march to their own beat. Spending time with one will challenge you to find yours."
—CosmoGIRL! editor

"Living your creative dreams renews your soul. Make time for them!"
—**SARK, author, illustrator**

97

"When I was younger, I kept my negative feelings in; I pleased people. And when you people-please, you please everyone but yourself. You dig yourself into a little cave. The only way out of that cave is to express yourself."
—Fergie, singer-songwriter

"We all need some time to let our emotions—instead of our heads—lead us. Have fun, and don't be afraid to live in the moment."
—Susan Schulz, CosmoGIRL! editor-in-chief

"Find ways to articulate whatever you're feeling as something constructive, whether it's art, music, sports or science."
—Eve Ensler, playwright, activist

"Imagination is about planting a seed of possibility in your own mind. After all, if you don't see it, how can you ever be it?"
—CosmoGIRL! editor

CG! LiFe TiPs

Inspiring Advice You Can Use Every Day!

You don't need to be like everyone else—those nutty bits of you that you may have written off as immature are the purest essence of who you are! Respect those parts and take the pressure off. Release your inner weirdo to the world and rejoice. You'll feel your soul sigh with relief.

Decide for yourself—and truly believe—that you're worth loving. Declare "From now on, no matter how tough life may be or how imperfect I may feel, I'm going to honestly love myself." Reward yourself for the person you are right now!

Make time for yourself. Time alone gets you in touch with your spirit. Your imagination can roam and you can come up with new ways to pursue your goals, so you can become the person you dream of being.

If you listen to your inner voice, you may learn that your version of happiness isn't anything like your friends or family. Be bold, and listen to that voice. Close the gap between the person who you are on the inside and who you seem to be on the outside.

COSMOgirl!

friends and family

Family can be a relative or a friend—it's someone who will always be there for you.

"If all my friends jumped off a cliff, I wouldn't jump off with them. But I would be at the bottom, ready to catch them."
—Heather, 15, CG! reader

"My mother always said to me, 'It's more important to be smart than beautiful.'"
—Nicole Kidman, actor

"I hate the word normal. My close friends look at me and say, 'You are a freak, and that's what I love about you!'"
—**Sandra Bullock, actor, producer**

"Secrets shared between friends are a sacred trust. Once you know a friend's deepest secrets, never use them as weapons in a fight."
—CosmoGIRL! editor

"My parents brought me up to believe that if I didn't get a job it was because it wasn't the right part for me—not that I was inadequate in some respect."

—Raven-Symone, actor

"When you are with a true friend, you are not afraid to be who you really are."

—Christa, 17, CG! reader

"If you have one GOOD friend, you're doing amazing for yourself."
—Summer, 19, CG! reader

"If your mom and dad don't get how mature you really are (because if they did, they'd let you do far more than they allow you to do now), then your job is to make them feel like they know you better."
—Jay McGraw, author

"My mother...loved me to death, and every time I was in a jam she was there for me—but she let me feel things out on my own and let me realize for myself how cold the world can be."
—Usher, singer, actor

"My sister and I are adopted. It's so sweet the way my mom describes it. She says that her kids weren't born under her heart but were born in it. I feel like we were all meant for each other."
—Lauren, 16, CG! reader

"My mom said, 'Don't be average. You are extraordinary, and if you settle for being just like everyone else, I'll be disappointed in you!'"
—Hilarie Burton, actor

"I freaked when my ex started dating my friend. Since I had no one to turn to, I turned to my mom. She really helped because she'd been through a similar experience. Sometimes parents truly can relate!"
—Natalie, 17, CG! reader

"My father…was a very hard-working person. The best advice he gave me was to just keep plugging. You can never stop. You can never give up. You can never say never."
—Donald Trump, businessman, television personality

"My mom always had me dance with her and open doors for her. She really wanted to make me into a gentleman."
—**Tyler Hilton, actor**

"Love + trust + care = real family!"
—Kelly, 15, CG! reader

> "My mom had always taught me to be independent in life and to rely on nobody but myself."
> —Skawenniio Barnes, CosmoGIRL! Born to Lead Award winner 2002

> "The best advice (my father has) given me is to trust my own vision and never let anyone stunt my creativity because it is my voice."
> —Katie Lucas, daughter of George Lucas, film director

"Family tries to teach you what they know, rather than leave you to figure it out on your own."
—Anne, 14, CG! reader

"I don't have girlfriends that are inconsiderate to other women. It's all about taking care of each other."
—Cameron Diaz, actor

"A journal can be like a great friend. You can tell it your deepest feelings and secrets...without it being all over school the next day."
—Tiara, 16, CG! reader

"My parents made sure I was on the right track and if I stayed out late, I'd get in trouble. So I have this boundary that's so ingrained in me. I want to know that I did everything I could—that I didn't spend years partying so much that I forgot about why I was here in the first place."
—Katie Holmes, actor

"I always go to my best friend for advice. She's comforting and she knows who I really am."
—**Amber Tamblyn, actor**

"Tough times are the proof of true friendship. And if the problem is in the friendship, real best friends teach each other how to forgive."
—CosmoGIRL! editor

"The best thing in the world is to laugh with a friend."
—Lyz, 16, CG! reader

"My mother was like, 'Never depend on anyone. Be self-sufficient because you can do whatever you want to do.' And now, I can live on my own, stand on my own. I don't need anyone to help me live."
—Jennifer Lopez, singer-songwriter, actor, designer

116

> "I think that sometimes we overestimate our parents' pressure. If you talk to them openly you might be surprised how much support they have for you."
> **—Jenny Ming, president of Old Navy**

> "Understanding what you really mean no matter what you say is a big part of friendship."
> Angelina, 18, CG! reader

"It's the everyday stuff that makes sister relationships so special. Even if you don't happen to have an actual sister, you can totally have these connections with your friends."
—**Susan Schulz,** CosmoGIRL! **editor-in-chief**

"I was the kind of kid who got super stressed out on grades and sports. My parents always told me, 'Don't do that to make us happy; make yourself happy first.' That advice led me to where I am today."
—Sam Page, actor

"**Friends are the best reflections of who you are.**"
—CosmoGIRL! **writer**

"I never felt it was a challenge to separate myself from my sister because we're so different. But I'd rather be compared to my sister than to anybody else. That's a huge compliment."

—Ashlee Simpson, singer-songwriter

"'Everything happens for a reason' is my mom's best advice. When one thing doesn't work out, something better does instead."

—Amanda Bynes, actor

"My mom always told me to just be myself and have fun, and as soon as I'm not having fun to reconsider things."
—Lindsay Lohan, actor, singer

"We've had a lot of personal struggles as a family and that's just made me realize how important family is. You can have all the money and power, but it's ultimately about the people in your life."
—Michael Copon, actor

"Anyone who will love you no matter what is family."
—Kriston, 17, CG! reader

"For me, sisterhood is all about respect."
—**Alexis Bledel, actor**

"Some people, if you're happy, are like, 'Man, what's that doing for me?' You need friends who have a good energy."
—Kanye West, hip-hop artist

"It's our best friends who first teach us how to be selfless—how to give the purest part of ourselves without the expectation of getting anything in return."
—CosmoGIRL! contributing writer

"The best friendships are something so sacred that a hug can say things better than words."
—Stephanie, 18 & Kayla, 21, CG! readers

"Always remember you deserve friends who respect and think about your feelings."
—**Susan Schulz,** CosmoGIRL! **editor-in-chief**

"No matter what happens, you can always go back to your family."
—Anonymous, 16, CG! reader

"The best friendships reserve time for each other but also respect the other people in each other's lives. Jealousy has no place."
—Heather, 17, CG! reader

"I love talking about him [my brother], and I love thinking about him. We've got to carry each other around through the world—and that's a good thing."
—Ashton Kutcher, actor

"I come from a family of really strong women, and they have taught me that you can't find your personal happiness in another human being. It's more important to be yourself and be with yourself."
—Brittany Murphy, actor

"Family is the cornerstone on which you build your own foundation."
—Kelly, 18, CG! reader

"Even if you're mad at each other, a true friend will never turn her back when you need them. There will be good times and bad times, but you're there for each other."
—Lety, 17, CG! reader

"Mom used to say, 'Don't preach—teach! Don't tell people what to do, but show them how to be.'"
—Johnathon Schaech, actor

"I feel totally free with my best friend because I can be myself—she doesn't expect anything else!"
—Sarah, 16, CG! reader

"The people you welcome into your world—your friends—define your life, and that's everything!"
—America Ferrera, actor

"Friends are the family you choose...so choose well!"
—Elizabeth, 15, CG! reader

"Life is like a roller coaster, having a best friend means that there's always someone beside you to scream, laugh, and hold your hand."

—CosmoGIRL! **editor**

"In your life you will have many friends; some will come and some will go. But you will always have your family."

—Malori, 17, CG! reader

"Mom always tells me that I shouldn't wish away the present by worrying about the future. I only live once, so every moment has to count."

—Katy, 17, CG! reader

"Relationships with parents can be hard to bear. You think, 'I'm my own person and I've got to learn on my own.' But as hard as it may be to listen, don't have too much pride. Choose your battles with your parents. They're only telling you because they care about you."
—Usher, singer, actor

"Always have a funny friend. They can cheer you up when you're down, plus they're never boring!"
—Glorelys, 15, CG! reader

CG! LiFe TiPS

Inspiring Advice You Can Use Every Day!

Learning to say you're sorry can save a friendship. Be specific about what you are sorry for, take responsibility and explain yourself. Let her know you understand her feelings and remind her about how special she is to you. Give her some time. A life-long friendship is totally worth it."

Being with your friends more doesn't mean you'll stop being close to your family—the bond you have with your family is too strong. But honor that bond by making sure you save time to do special things with your family, so you can enjoy all the people in your life!

Bonding with your mom happens every day in little ways. But it's important to take a whole day—at least once in a while!—to just enjoy time with each other to honor that bond. Spending a little girl time with your mom won't just make her feel good, it will make you feel great too!

You have the power to seek out the types of people you want to fill your life with. If you choose wisely, your future will be filled with people who will value and support you.

COSMO girl!

tough stuff

{ *If something in your life is hard to get through, then the reward at the end is probably worth it. Going through difficult times defines who you are and makes you stronger.* }

> **"I take care of myself because I learned early on that I'm the only person who's responsible for me."**
> **—Halle Berry, actor**

"I….had to learn what forgiveness really meant. I used to tell people, 'I forgive you'—but I didn't feel it until I started forgiving myself….So now, each night, I write down three things I'm grateful for and three things I need to forgive myself for."
—Alanis Morissette, singer-songwriter

"Love your enemies, for they tell you your faults."
—**Benjamin Franklin, inventor**

"It is easier to fix a small problem than it is to wait and try to fix it when it's a big one."
—Meagan, 18, CG! reader

"I never want to be stagnant and comfortable...change is a good thing."
—Jennifer Aniston, actor

"Every breakup is painful—whether it's a boyfriend or your parents' marriage."
—**Lindsay Lohan, actor, singer**

"Don't stick your hand in the piranha tank just so the fish will like you."
—Courtney, 15, CG! reader

"Just because you've been a victim once, doesn't mean that's the role you have to stay in. One day you'll be free."
—Susan Schulz, CosmoGIRL! editor-in-chief

"Never fear shadows. They simply mean there's a light shining somewhere nearby."
—Samantha, 21, CG! reader

"Talking to someone—a friend, a parent, school counselor—helps. You need to find someone who has a positive opinion and positive views."
—Christina Milian, singer, actor

"When you live your life afraid to die, you're afraid to live."
—50 Cent, rapper

"Stand up for what you believe in, even if it seems impossible."
—Hannah, 15, CG! reader

"I have thick skin—I don't like sugarcoating."
—Eve, singer

"The happiest people don't have the best of everything, they just make the best out of whatever comes their way."
—Minnie, 16, CG! reader

"My limbs work, so I'm not going to complain about the way my body is shaped."
—**Drew Barrymore, actor, producer**

"Use your disadvantages to your advantage."
—Ruthie, 16, CG! reader

"I refuse to let someone else's negativity have a part in the way I feel about my life."
—Jennifer Lopez, singer-songwriter, actor, designer

"If I don't stand for something, I'll fall for anything."
—Zsa Zsa, 15, CG! reader

"...being laughed at made me want to prove myself—and it made me look at my flaws and try to better myself."
—**Jessica Simpson, singer, actor**

"I would rather be hated for who I am than loved for someone I'm not!"
—Taylor, 15, CG! reader

143

"You can be sad…but you're still strong by being able to show that emotion."
—**Alicia Keys, singer-songwriter**

"When all else fails, you have to help yourself. Hold onto reality, hope, faith, dreams…hold onto whatever makes you happy."
—Amanda, 14, CG! reader

"**Everybody can't be the Terminator; you've got to lose sometimes.**"
—**Jay-Z, singer-songwriter, record executive**

"Use every challenge as an inspiration to be more successful."
—Candace, 15, CG! reader

"I learned that you can deal with reality and still have fun. Everything shouldn't be so serious all the time. I like to enjoy life and I want to continue to always enjoy it."
—Nicole Richie, television personality

145

"**Nobody is perfect all the time, and if you're trying to keep that act up, it's exhausting.**"
—**Drew Barrymore, actor, producer**

"Stay strong, let it pass...bad times never last."
— Nina, 19, CG! reader

"Trust your own instincts and don't apologize for them, because they're yours and they come from a good place."
— Anne Hathaway, actor

"I don't think there are seven deadly sins—there is just one: fear."
—**Erykah Badu, singer-songwriter**

"When one door closes, another opens and it's our job to find that door."
—Matthew Perry, actor

"It's okay to stick your foot in your mouth. Just laugh at yourself with everybody else."
—**Jessica Simpson, singer, actor**

"We learn the best lessons from the mistakes we thought were the worst."
—Gina, 18, CG! reader

"Strength doesn't come from winning. Your struggles develop your strengths."
—Arnold Schwarzenegger, actor, politician

"Nobody is tough and strong all the time. To say that is to deny human emotion."
—Liv Tyler, actor

"We are sometimes taken into troubled waters not to drown, but to be cleansed."
—Ashley, 16, CG! reader

"When people pick on you, it's usually because you have something they don't have. If you're smart and they're not, they're going to dog you. If you've got pretty hair and they don't, they're gonna try to tear you down."
—Kelly Rowland, singer

> **"You can get past anything, no matter how severe."**
> **—L.L. Cool J, musician, actor**

"No matter who you are or what you do, you're always going to have doubters. There's nothing you can do about it, so get over it and don't even let it bother you."
—Nelly, singer

> **"I think people are perfect in their imperfections."**
> **—Jessica Alba, actor**

"You might not be happy in the moment, but if you stay true to yourself, you'll be happy in the end."
—Rose McGowan, actor

"The truth leaves a repairable cut, but a lie leaves a jagged wound. It doesn't readily heal."
—Will Smith, actor, singer

"Life's about messing up and getting on your feet again."
—**Debra Messing, actor**

"Everything happens for a reason, even though you haven't figured out the reason yet."
—Anja, 16, CG! reader

"I prefer an ugly truth to a pretty lie. If someone is telling me the truth, that is when I give my heart."
—Shakira, singer-songwriter

> "Whenever you see darkness, there is extraordinary opportunity for the light to burn brighter."
> —**Bono, singer-songwriter, humanitarian**

> "Don't look at how your life is now and feel it's going to be that way forever."
> —Barbara Walters, journalist

> "Nothing beats frustration like singing your brains out to loud music."
> —Liz, 17, CG! reader

153

"People say that you're going the wrong way when it's simply a way of your own."
—Angelina Jolie, actor, humanitarian

"No one else holds power over you. You have the power to change things if you're unhappy."
—Brittany Murphy, actor

"I don't believe in regret. Even if something turns out negatively, you can learn from that situation."
—Eve, rapper

"I have not failed. I've just found 10,000 ways that don't work."
—Thomas Edison, inventor

"Confidence will make you a powerful person."
—Alexia, 18, CG! reader

"I've learned that it's okay—sometimes—to avoid your problems until you're ready to deal with them, and to avoid things at certain times and embrace them at others."
—Shia LaBeouf, actor

"Say to yourself: 'I'm great.' Believe it and you can get through anything."
—Hannah, 16, CG! reader

> "Complaining alone does nothing. You have to methodically work on solving the problem."
> —Stephanie Varlotta, CosmoGIRL! Born to Lead Award winner 2002

> "The truth is, bad things do happen in this world and you should know how to open up a can of whoop-ass if you ever need it."
> —Erin Weed, CosmoGIRL! Born to Lead Award winner 2002

"There are always going to be bumps. Figuring out how to get over the bumps—that's what's really fun."
—Alicia Silverstone, actor

"Cry it out if you need to. It's one less emotion weighing you down."
—Angela, 17, CG! reader

> **"When you're forced to stand alone, you realize what you have in you."**
> **—Uma Thurman, actor**

"Just around every corner there's always a new beginning, someone to care about you and help you."
—Terry Iacuzzo, psychic, CosmoGIRL! contributor

"I have realized that violence will never solve anything. Hurting someone will not make things better—it will only cause more tension and more violence."
—Katy, 18, CG! reader

"People's words affect you only as much as you let them. You know who you are. Focus on that. Other people will see that eventually."
—Jennifer Lopez, singer-songwriter, actor, designer

> "The best fight is the one never fought."
> —Erin Weed, CosmoGIRL! **Born to Lead Award winner 2002**

"People aren't mean because they want to make you feel bad—it's usually because they're ignorant."
—Jennifer Jernigan, CosmoGIRL! Born to Lead Award winner 2003

161

"Learn to see more than one side—it will help you find your way."
—Emma, 15, CG! reader

"You don't get everything you want anyway, so why fight for everything? Just save it for things you really need."
—Clay Aiken, singer-songwriter, American Idol finalist

"I find the less you focus on your flaws, the better off you are. Be yourself, and be glad."
—**Michelle Pfeiffer, actor**

"Always get it off your chest!"
—Shaina, 16, CG! reader

Inspiring Advice You Can Use Every Day!

If venting to a friend, pouring out your feelings in a journal, and exercising don't seem to helping you get through the hard emotional times, professional help is an option. Make it a point to check in with yourself on a regular basis.

The best thing about our best days is that they give us hope and strength to get through the tough times. No matter how bad things get, you know you've had great days, and you will have them again.

Chronic stress can lead to depression or anxiety—especially it you keep it to yourself. Girls often blame themselves for whatever's causing their stress. If you're feeling overwhelmed, the best thing to do is talk about it.

COSMO girl!

dream it, be it

{ *Every one of us has the potential to be a leader. Every single one of us has the potential to do great things. You are Born to Lead your life, your way!* }

"It's just as important to find out what you don't want to do as what you do want to do."
—Brad Pitt, actor

"There's always going to be another wall to climb over….I'll never give it less than 100%"
—Queen Latifah, singer, actor

"People who daydream know how to imagine the possibilities."
—Kalsay, 15, CG! reader

"If I feel it in my gut, I just leap...If you fall down, you figure it out for the next time."

—Justin Timberlake, singer-songwriter

"If I see a door comin' my way, I'm knocking it down. And if I can't...I'm sliding through the window."

—Rosie Perez, actor

"I have a list of 50 things I want to achieve. Life's fragility drives me."

—Amy Lee, singer-songwriter

"Don't let anybody tell you how hard it is. Just do it."

—Nia Vardalos, screenwriter, actor

"People say the sky's the limit. I believe in Master P's phrase: There is NO LIMIT—bump the sky out of the way!"

—Gariarta, 15, CG! reader

"Nobody made a greater mistake than he who did nothing because he could only do a little."
—**Edmund Burke, scholar**

"It isn't where you come from; it's where you're going that counts."
—Ella Fitzgerald, jazz legend

"I'm not going to talk about anything until I do it."
—**Natalie Portman, actor**

"There's this wonderful quality that most successful people have…You have to believe in the impossible."
—**Will Smith, actor**

"The only limits are the limits of our imagination. Dream up the kind of world you want to live in."
—Bono, singer-songwriter, humanitarian

"Go big or go home. Because it's true: What do you have to lose?"
—**Eliza Dushku, actor**

"Being the best is a simple decision…It's about commitment, plain and simple."
—**Mia Hamm, athlete**

"God gives everybody gifts—you just have to realize what yours is and work on that."
—Beyoncé Knowles, singer, actor

"A winner often proves everyone wrong."
—**Tara Lipinski, athlete**

"If I didn't have some kind of education, I wouldn't be able to count my money."
—Missy Elliott, musician

"One of my rules is, Never try anything—just do it."
—Ani DiFranco, singer-songwriter

"I don't want to be the next somebody. I want to be the first me."
—Emille, 15, CG! reader

"You have to learn what you're good at and what you're not good at, and figure out how to help yourself."

—**Bobbi Brown, makeup artist**

"If you want something bad enough, you shall receive it if you believe it hard enough."

—Angelina, 18, CG! reader

175

"When you figure out what you want to do take your interest and your talent seriously. Spend all the time you can developing your skills and getting experience. If something goes wrong, ask questions so you can do it better next time!"

—Rocco DiSpirito, celebrity chef

"Mean people don't succeed."

—Paris Hilton, celebrity

"Credit is something to be given, not to be taken."

—Pharrell Williams, singer

"Sometimes the noise of success can block out the sound of your heart. So listen to it—it's what got you there in the first place."
—CosmoGIRL! editor

"That's the coolest thing in the world, to have success from you being you."
—Jessica Simpson, singer, actor

"Believe in yourself when no one else does. That makes you a winner right there."
—Venus Williams, athlete

"I've had the same goal since I was a girl. I want to rule the world."
—**Madonna, singer-songwriter, actor**

"Have a passion for what you're doing….if you don't love it, you will never be successful."
—Donald Trump, businessman

"All the nay-sayers in my life pissed me off. But they've given me unstoppable ambition."
—**Tobey Maguire, actor**

"Success isn't about material things or stuff outside yourself, it's about a satisfaction you feel within yourself."
—Jay McGraw, author

"People judge you by your actions, not by your intentions. You may have a heart of gold, but so does a hard-boiled egg."
—Kiran, 15, CG! reader

"If it's something I believe in, I have to do it. If I fail at it, that's my fault, and I'll live with that."
—Jennifer Love-Hewitt, actor, singer

"**What's more satisfying is the struggle rather than sitting back and relishing achievement.**"
—Ben Affleck, actor

"If you put yourself in the position to fail, to try something you've never done, that's when you learn the most."
—Ethan Hawke, actor

180

"It's bizarre when your dreams become reality...[So] I have this paper taped to my phone that reads 'Dream Bigger.'"
—Ashton Kutcher, actor

"Have some idea, not about what you want to do, but about the kind of person you want to be."
—Barbara Walters, journalist

"If you're going to be thinking anyway, you might as well think big."
—Donald Trump, businessman

"There's nothing you can be that is better than yourself. Copying anybody else will only make you second best."
—Sharon Stone, actor

"Whether you think you can or think you can't—you're right."
—Henry Ford, American industrialist

"You may be disappointed if you fail, but you are doomed if you don't try."
—Beverly Sills, opera singer

"People laughed at the way I was dressed, but that was the secret of my success: I didn't look like anyone."
—Coco Chanel, fashion designer

"Opportunities are usually disguised as hard work, so most people don't recognize them."
—Ann Landers, advice columnist

183

"Eighty percent of success is showing up."
—Woody Allen, director

"I don't know the key to success, but the key to failure is trying to please everybody."
—Bill Cosby, comedian

"By being willing to be a bad artist, you have a chance to be an artist."
—Julia Cameron, artist, writer

"If there is a book you really want to read, but it hasn't been written yet, then you must write it."
—**Toni Morrison, author**

"Don't dream it, be it."
—Dr. Frank N. Furter (Tim Curry) in The Rocky Horror Picture Show

"The time when you need to do something is when…people are saying it can't be done."
—Mary Frances Berry, civil rights activist

"You miss 100 percent of the shots you don't take."
—Wayne Gretzky, athlete

"Our doubts are traitors and make us lose the good we oft might win by fearing to attempt."
—William Shakespeare, poet, playwright

"Getting what you go after is success, but liking it while you're getting it is happiness."
—**Bertha Damon, author**

"It's important not to fear trouble. You cannot be a leader if you do not embrace problems....Have the confidence in yourself that you will figure it out."
—Elaine Chao, U.S. Secretary of Labor

"If you're worrying about the competition, you don't focus enough on what you're doing."
—Katie Couric, television personality, author

"Whatever your dream may be, someone will say you can't do it—and you have to know you can."
—Rosie O'Donnell, entertainer

"Only when you really give yourself up can you make great art."
—Shirley Manson, singer-songwriter

> "My response to adversity is always the same: work harder."
> **—Janet Jackson, singer**

> "Rather than focusing on your weaknesses, spend your time developing your strengths. Knowing you're good at things will help you accept that you can excel at everything."
> —Dan Baker, Ph.D., author

> "The simple act of paying attention can take you a long way."
> **—Keanu Reeves, actor**

"If you love it, do it. If you don't love it, leave it alone."
—Mariah Carey, singer

"Never doubt that a small group of thoughtful, committed citizens can change the world."
—Margaret Mead, sociologist

190

"Surround yourself with people who have the same work ethic, passion, and goals as you. If you're surrounded by people who don't, then become the person who inspires them to have it."
—Will.I.Am, musician

"All the skepticism just made me more passionate. I've always faced people who doubted me by working even harder to prove them wrong."
—Diana Taurasi, guard, Phoenix Mercury basketball team

CG! LiFe TiPs

Inspiring Advice You Can Use Every Day!

When someone says "You'd be great at
_____," file it away in your memory or
write it down (even if you don't agree).
Ask people what they think you'd be
good at. Others might see things in you
that you might not yet see in yourself.
You might just hear something that
sounds good!

Happy and successful people keep a
balance in their lives between family,
friends, school, and time for themselves,
so if one thing isn't going their way, there
are lots of other things that are.

Make sure you have direct control over your dream and it's not something based on others' decisions. (Like you are in charge of being outgoing, but you're not in charge of winning Most Popular.) Goals that you control put you in command of your life. Now that's power!

Each of us has a unique gift to offer. And if you have the desire to share it, the focus to develop it, and the tenacity to stick with it, any doubts you may have about what your gift is will melt away.

COSMO girl!

life
lessons

{ *Life can only be understood backwards; but it must be lived forwards.* }

"Life is ours to be spent, not to be saved."
—D.H. Lawrence, author

"You've gotta believe you'll get good waves, but it's also good to just sit on the surfboard and enjoy the sun."
—Charlize Theron, actor

"Never fail to know that if you are doing all the talking, you are boring somebody."
—**Helen Gurley Brown, author, publisher, editor-in-chief of the international editions of** Cosmopolitan

"Nothing comes without hard work and a good attitude."
—Lindsay, 18, CG! reader

197

"Look at changes, like friends moving away, not as a loss, but as a shift. Think of it as people "moving on" but not "leaving you behind." The positivity puts you in control."
—Susan Schulz, CosmoGIRL! editor-in-chief

"Fear less, hope more; eat less, chew more; whine less, breathe more; talk less, say more; love more, and all good things will be yours."
—Swedish proverb

"I think the thing to do in life is to enjoy the ride while you're on it."
—Johnny Depp, actor

"People's impressions of you aren't always right. People used to look at me and think I was too young or too geeky to know what I was doing. They would underestimate me, and that created opportunities."
—Mark Cuban, self-made billionaire

"You really do only live once...try to make the most of every moment (you've) got."
—Julie, 17, CG! reader, accident survivor

"My life, my freedom, my chance to enjoy every day, is much more important than aspiring to unrealistic and unhealthy goals."
—CosmoGIRL! contributing writer

"Life is too short to let a bad hair day get you down."
—**Brittany Murphy, actor**

"Listen more than you speak."
—Melissa, 20, CG! reader

"The purpose of life is to have a life of purpose."
—Frances, 20, CG! reader

"You can't do your best work by working, working, working and not living life at all."
—Kirsten Dunst, actor

"Take your chances doing things that may look crazy to other people."
—**Oprah Winfrey**

"You will never know where life will take you."
—Ashlee Simpson, singer-songwriter

"I believe in the philosophy of the present—in living right now."
—**Jennifer Lopez, singer-songwriter, actor, designer**

"Playing on a team is like being on a journey together where you all have a common goal. And I honestly believe that if you do your best, good things will happen for the whole team."
—Sue Bird, guard, Seattle Storm basketball team

"Only you can decide what choices are right for you. Make decisions that you respect, and you will lead an ethical life!"
—CosmoGIRL! editor

"Don't compromise yourself. You're all you've got."
—Janis Joplin, musician

"Never regret anything that made you smile!"
—Katherine, 15, CG! reader

"I discovered I always have choices and sometimes it's only a choice of attitude."
—Judith M. Knowlton, author

"If you obey all the rules, you miss all the fun."
—Katharine Hepburn, actor

"It's easy to make a buck. It's a lot tougher to make a difference."
—Tom Brokaw, journalist

"Sometimes it's your day, sometimes it's not. No [one] wins all the time."
—Michelle Kwan, athlete

"The way I see it, if you want the rainbow, you gotta put up with the rain."
—Dolly Parton, entertainer

"I didn't have to become rich and famous to have a happy ending. I have food and a house—that's success."
—Shania Twain, singer-songwriter

"I have learned that you can make a mistake, and the world doesn't end."
—Lisa Kudrow, actor

"'I can't' really means 'I won't.'"
—Melissa, 23, CG! reader

"If one person gets involved, it can change things. If we don't get involved in small ways it can lead to our future downfall. I know we can make a difference."
—Lexi, 15, CG! reader

"You can have all the things you want to have in life if you feel good about yourself."
—Lucy Liu, actor

"I've never waited for anyone to give me anything. I'm of the mind that I'll just get to do it myself."
—Vin Diesel, actor

"If you don't have good stories to tell on your deathbed, what good was living?"
—Sandra Bullock, actor, producer

"Black or white or gay or straight—a good person is just a good person."
—**The Rock, actor**

"If you always do what you've always done, you'll only get what you already have."
—Vicki, 21, CG! reader

"If you do things from your heart, it all falls into place."
—Bernie Mac, actor, comedian

"Clarity always comes, so you just have to be patient. You have to have faith that you're on the right path and it will all work out."
—Katie Holmes, actor

"There's more to life than cheekbones."
—Kate Winslet, actor

"Be on time. Look people in the eye. Be nice."
—Bobbi Brown, makeup artist

"A sense of humor usually goes hand in hand with smarts and confidence. You need confidence to be funny."
—**Adam Brody, actor**

"If you wake up deciding what you want to give versus what you're going to get, you become a more successful person. Which of your special talents can you give to the world?"
—Russell Simmons, hip-hop mogul

"Even though we all want to be liked by everyone, that's just not going to happen, and girls shouldn't worry about that. They have to make themselves happy first."
—Lindsay Lohan, actor, singer

"All positive change in the world begins with one person. Why can't it be you?"
— CosmoGIRL!
contributing writer

"Struggle is good because it keeps you persevering, and one day you'll look at yourself and see how much character you've developed."
—Jessica Simpson, actor, singer

"The path to happiness doesn't start with a boyfriend, a good grade or even a million dollars. True happiness starts with you."
—Dan Baker, Ph.D., author

"If you take in other people's negativity, then you're doing nothing but tearing yourself down. Instead, fight harder. Work harder. Prove them wrong."
—Fantasia Barrino, CosmoGIRL! Born to Lead Award winner 2004

"You know what happens when you're healthy? You feel confident, you feel strong, and guess what? You look—you are—beautiful."
— CosmoGIRL! staff writer

"You want to be able to get up in the morning and think about the good you're doing in the world. There's a lot more to life than having a fast car and a big house."

—Marsha Evans, head of the American Red Cross

"We all make mistakes. The key is to learn from them."

—Jennifer Lopez, singer-songwriter, actor, designer

"You learn a lot going from 17 to 19. And I'm still learning who I am."
—**Avril Lavigne, singer-songwriter**

"We are responsible for our actions; we do have a choice."
—Stacey, 19, CG! reader

"If you don't get out of the box that you've been raised in, you won't understand how much bigger the world is—and what is truly real."
—Angelina Jolie, actor, humanitarian

"If you're so worried about what everyone around you is thinking, they see it—it's written all over your face. And if you're happy inside, people respect it. Make that choice inside to be happy."
—Nikki Reed, 16, screenwriter of Thirteen, CosmoGIRL! Born to Lead Award winner 2003

"Amazing experiences only come your way when you decide to be open to them."
—Ann, 22, CG! reader

CG! LiFe TiPs

Say it out loud: I accept that change is part of life. I will embrace change as it comes and will seek what is positive about it. As I change, I grow. As I grow, I become a better me.

No one is perfect, and accepting that it's okay to make mistakes and ask for help if you need it is liberating. You can't always be in control, and things will be all right even if you're not!

You will find people in your life that you just don't really like. But be nice to them and just move on. Taking the high road means that no matter what, you're known as the girl who's always nice to be around—and make you proud to know that you're a bigger, more gracious person than most.

Ultimately, you have to be your own best ally—someone who takes care of herself so she can have the life she wants and deserves.

index